The Si

FRIEI
NIETZSCHE

edited by

ROBERT PEARCE

Duckworth Overlook

Also available in *The Sayings* series:

The Sayings of

FRIEDRICH
NIETZSCHE

edited by

ROBERT PEARCE

Duckworth Overlook

This edition and eBook
first published in the UK in 2013 by
Duckworth Overlook

LONDON
30 Calvin Street, London E1 6NW
T: 020 7490 7300
E: info@duckworth-publishers.co.uk
www.ducknet.co.uk
For bulk and special sales please contact
sales@duckworth-publishers.co.uk,
or write to us at the above address.

NEW YORK
141 Wooster Street
New York, NY 10012
www.overlookpress.com

Introduction and editorial arrangement
© 1993 by Stoddard Martin

A catalogue record for this book is available
from the British Library

ISBNs
Paperback: 9780715624753
Kindle: 9780715648001
ePub: 9780715648018
Library PDF: 9780715648025

Printed in the UK by
CPI Group (UK) Limited, Croydon CR0 4YY

Contents

Introduction

The received prejudice among those who have not read him is that Nietzsche was a forerunner of the Nazis. In fact, as the aphorisms in this book show, he despised the state, disparaged the Germans, admired the Jews, and believed in the individual. It is chiefly in temperament that a connection might be made to the political fanatics of the early twentieth century. Nietzsche was addicted to great passions. He believed that to annihilate was to create. Monomaniacal in pursuit of truth (though regularly protesting that it could not be found), he granted little sympathy to cant of any kind and was ruthlessly hard on himself. All forms of weakness were anathema to him. Strength of will became a faith. Triumph over illness, decadence, adversity – this was the message. The medium, however, was the man of thought, not of action: the solitary who loved life, yet condemned the mob; above all the critic poised to pounce on error, his own or others – the self-detector, castigator, genuine ironist.

Academic policemen of the 'politically correct' accuse Nietzsche of being a principal source of modern elitism. Inasmuch as he yearned for man to pass beyond the 'human, all-too-human', this is just. Though recognising that mediocrity has its place in wider culture, he was wildly partisan to the exceptional. He knew the cost in human suffering individual greatness entailed and believed that nothing new or glorious could be created without it. For academic witch-hunters opposed to the free play of genius, he would have nothing but an Olympian laugh. He had a name for them: Culture Philistines. These establishment censors in disguise – philologists, academic time-servers, ersatz critical theorists – struck him as parasites on the body of true culture. Along with journalists, they were the secret enemies of Beauty and Greatness – the Platonic ideals toward which he was drawn, yet whose existence he felt compelled to deny because of his remorseless scepticism.

Nietzsche began his adult career as a lecturer in classics at the University of Basle. His father had been a Lutheran pastor who died of a brain disorder perhaps caused by syphilis when Nietzsche was less than five. Out of this background, the young man developed a loathing for the hypocrisies of the church, combined with the ascetic character of a priest – indeed, a monk or a saint. He joined the army briefly during the period of German unification, but bad eyesight and chronic headaches made him unable to serve for more than a few months. These debilities worsened under the self-induced stress of writing and led to his resignation from his academic post in his early thirties. Ten years of wandering followed, through Switzerland, southern Germany, Italy and the Côte d'Azur. Unable to find a spot conducive to restoring his health, he lived in boarding houses and train compartments, ever on the run, waging his 'skirmishes in a war with the age' in the sketches and half-essays which became his literary style. At the age of forty-four he had a complete mental breakdown. Tradition ascribes this to tertiary syphilis, either inherited from his father or contracted from a prostitute when he was a university student. The evidence, however, is inconclusive.

It is possible that Nietzsche never had proper sexual intercourse in his life. If he did, it could not have occurred more than a few times. Wagner, uncharitably, attributed his solipsism and illness to excessive masturbation – a charge for which there is no corroboration either. What is undeniable is that Nietzsche became increasingly obsessed with a sort of supermale hardness and exaltation of a kind which prefigures the 'phallic consciousness' of D.H. Lawrence or even the 'erotic reality' which Herbert Marcuse would promulgate for 'free spirits' of the 1960s. In his enthusiasm for Life with a capital 'L', Nietzsche is an important precursor of these movements. With them, he shared contempt for bourgeois ease and intellectual mendacity. But though he took opium and chloral-hydrate for his headaches, we cannot associate him with the drug-craziness and sexual excess of some of his apparent successors, any more than with the race-hatred and mass carnage of the Nazis. Again, Nietzsche was a man of thought and an ascetic, not an overt actor or indulger.

Nietzsche's resignation from his chair in philology was contemporary with his passion for and apostasy from the cult of Richard Wagner. For the young Nietzsche, the composer-dramatist was a substitute for the father he had never known; for the maturing philosopher, the 'Cagliostro of Bayreuth' became a titanic precursor who had to be overthrown. In Nietzsche's intellectual development, Schopenhauer shared this position with Wagner; but it was Schopenhauer-via-Wagner and Wagner himself to whom he returned again and again. Nietzsche's first book, *The Birth of Tragedy out of the Spirit of Music,* was written in a spell of euphoria for the Wagnerian *Gesamtkunstwerk* as a successor to the highest achievements of the Greeks. His most extensive, personal and characteristic work, *Human, All-too-Human,* was written in reaction against the coterie of nationalists, anti-Semites and dilettantes gathered around Wagner at Bayreuth. His last, fragmentary works written before his breakdown included *The Case of Wagner* and *Nietzsche contra Wagner.*

Seldom has a relationship in arts and letters proved so fateful. Against Wagner, Nietzsche was able to measure and define most of the issues which concerned him. In aesthetics, where the 'Meister' embraced totality and dark tones, Nietzsche came to extol detail and lightness of touch. In religion, where the creator of *Parsifal* relaxed into a vague synthesis of Christianity and Buddhism, Nietzsche remained an iconoclast and devotee of the Life-force. In morality and politics, where Wagner began truly to prefigure the Nazis, Nietzsche became a committed pan-European and partisan of the international free spirit. Yet despite these differences, Nietzsche shared with Wagner to the end an overwhelming attraction to the heroic, the transcendental, the eternal and the mythic; to the glorification of genius, its untrammelled self-expression, its *super*-humanness. He was allergic to the quotidian and simple. In this respect, his enthusiasm for Life inevitably leads, as did Wagnerism, towards a renunciation of life as we know it.

Through his most famous persona, the hermit-sage Zarathustra, Nietzsche explains that he could never marry because he was wedded to eternity. For a time during the creation of that persona, he was in love with the Russian *femme savante / femme fatale* Lou Andreas-Salomé, who later became intimate with Freud. Nietzsche seems to have proposed marriage to Lou and to have been rejected. He seems also to have dreamed of setting up a ménage with her and their mutual friend, the Jewish psychologist Paul Rée. At other times, he enthused about forming a community of advanced thinkers, gathering disciples around him in a manner not unlike Wagner at Bayreuth. But as a man, Nietzsche was increasingly unable to cope with human relationships. Apart from the friends and acquaintances who came to read to him when he was almost blind, his last years are a tale of increasing remoteness. At last, following his breakdown, he was taken care of by his sister Elisabeth, who had married one of the most notorious anti-Semites of the day and set about to ensure that her brother's memory would have prominence in the pantheon of the Nazis.

This disservice has in recent years been undone. That it ever occurred is a testimony to the daring with which post-Nietzschean Germany was able, in his phrase, to 'transvalue all values'. But the Nietzsche we find in the eighteen volumes published under his own supervision is anything but an apologist for narrow German *Wille-zur-Macht*. He claimed proudly to be Polish by blood, citing his father's name and a somewhat Slavic aspect to his forehead and face. Among European traditions, he felt that the French had most to offer; and in style and substance he has been justly described as a cross between La Rochefoucauld and Freud. The country he loved best was Italy; the country he lived in most was Switzerland; the landscape where he felt most alive was the shore of the Mediterranean. In identifying his kind he used the formula, 'We Europeans, We Immoralists, We Free Spirits'. This we should accept; and within such a sodality, he remains the characteristic voice. If his life and work exhibit more pain and passion than successors of our day might find congenial, it may be simply

because he was the necessary forerunner, as he claimed
– the pregnant great spirit screaming as he gives birth to
a substantially New Age.

Sources

The Birth of Tragedy, 1871
The Future of Our Educational Institutions, 1872
Early Greek Philosophy, 1873
Thoughts Out of Season, I ('David Strauss'; 'Uses and Abuses of
    History'), 1873
We Philologists, 1875
Thoughts Out of Season, II ('Schopenhauer'; 'Wagner'), 1874-6
Human, All-too-Human, I, 1877
Human, All-too-Human, II ('The Wanderer and His Shadow'),
    1878-9
The Dawn of Day, 1880
The Gay Science, 1881-2
Thus Spake Zarathustra, 1883-4
Beyond Good and Evil, 1885-6
A Genealogy of Morals ('People and Countries'), 1887
The Case of Wagner, 1888
The Twilight of the Idols, 1888
The Antichrist, 1888
Ecce Homo, 1888
Nietzsche contra Wagner, 1888
The Will to Power (unfinished)

Translations are taken for the most part from the first complete
edition of Nietzsche in English, published between 1909 and
1913. This is the edition that would have been available to the
writers in English most influenced by Nietzsche, such as Yeats,
Pound, Shaw, Lawrence, Wyndham Lewis and Jack London.
Some emendations for style have been made. The sources give
references to the sections of each work, not to the page
numbers of a specific edition.

Aesthetics

The existence of the world is justified only as an aesthetic phenomenon.

Birth of Tragedy, 'An Attempt at Self-Criticism', 5

Life is worth living, says art, the beautiful temptress. Life is worth knowing, says science.

'David Strauss, Confessor', VIII, *Thoughts Out of Season*, I

Art is the business of the man who is re-creating himself.

'Wagner at Bayreuth', IV, *Ibid.*

One must guess the painter in order to understand the picture.

'Schopenhauer as Educator', III, *Thoughts Out of Season*, II

There should be a *police des moeurs* in charge of bad pianists who play Beethoven.

We Philologists, 174

Artists are the glorifiers of humanity's religious and philosophical errors.

Human, All-too-Human, I, 220

The scientific man is a further development of the artistic man.

Ibid., 222

As in old age we recall our youth and celebrate festivals of memory, so in a short time mankind will stand in relation to art. It will be no more than a touching memory of the joys of the youth of the race.

Ibid., 224

The man who doesn't have the courage to allow himself and his work to be considered tedious is certainly no intellect of the first rank, whether in the arts or the sciences.

Ibid., II, 25

A work that is meant to give an impression of health should be produced at three-quarters of the strength of its creator … All good things have something lazy about them and lie like cows in the meadow.

Ibid., 107

The baroque style always arises at the time of decay of a great art. *Ibid.*, 144

Among all products of the artistic sense, ideas are the most solid and lasting. *Ibid.*, 171

He that prefers the beautiful to the useful will undoubtedly, like a child who prefers sweets to bread, destroy his digestion and acquire a fretful outlook. *Ibid.*, 364

The grand style comes into being when the beautiful wins a victory over the monstrous.

'The Wanderer and His Shadow', 96

The temptation to traverse forbidden paths and have a say in science as well is forgivable in the artist. Even the ablest craftsman at times finds his workshop unendurable.

Ibid., 123

The desire to display more sentiment than one feels corrupts style. *Ibid.*, 136

Artists are night-walkers by day. *Gay Science*, 59

It is of little importance what the philosophy of an artist is, provided that it does not do any injury to his art.

Ibid., 99

Let us not forget that all artists are actors of a sort. They could not hold out in the long run without stage-playing.

Ibid.

The artist chooses his subjects. That is his mode of praising.
Ibid., 245

The melancholia of everything *completed*! *Ibid.*, 277

Masters of the first rank are recognized by the fact that they know how to find a perfect end: be it the end of a melody or of a thought, the fifth act of a tragedy or of an affair of state.
Ibid., 281

What is it that gives a meaning, a value, an importance to things? The creative heart which yearns and which created out of this yearning.

Thus Spake Zarathustra, unpublished notes, 68

Our religion, morality and philosophy are decadent human
institutions. The counter-agent? Art.   *Will to Power*, 794

In all creative artists, productiveness ceases at the same time as
sexual potency does.

Ibid., 800

Absolute beauty exists just as little as absolute goodness and
truth.   *Ibid.*, 804

It is an honour for an artist to have no critical faculty. If he can
criticize, he is mediocre; he is *modern*.

Ibid., 811

The inartistic states are: objectivity, resignation, suspension of
the will.   *Ibid.*, 812

Art is with us in order that we might not perish through truth.
Ibid., 822

A romanticist is an artist whose great dissatisfaction with
himself makes him productive.   *Ibid.*, 844

With every individual artwork I ask, has hunger or
superabundance created this?

Ibid., 846

All that is good is easy; everything divine runs with light feet.
Case of Wagner, 1

It is easier to be titanic than to be beautiful.   *Ibid.*, 6

Expressiveness at all costs, the ideal of decadence, is not
compatible with talent.   *Ibid.*, 11

Artists very often do not know what they do best. They are
much too vain.

Nietzsche contra Wagner, I

Religion

People whose daily life appears empty and monotonous easily grow religious. This is comprehensible and excusable; but they have no right to demand religious sentiments from those whose daily life is not empty and monotonous.

Human, All-too-Human, I, 115

Christianity arose for the purpose of lightening the heart; but now it must first make the heart heavy in order to lighten it. Consequently it will perish. *Ibid.*, 119

There is not sufficient love and goodness in the world to permit us to give some of it away to imaginary beings.

Ibid., 129

In every ascetic morality, man worships one part of himself as a God and is obliged therefore to diabolize the other parts.

Ibid., 137

Regarding the chastity of saints – it is easier to give up a desire entirely than to keep it within bounds. *Ibid.*, 139

The best way to begin a day well might be to think on waking whether one can give pleasure to at least one person. If this could become a substitute for the religious habit of prayer, our fellow-men would benefit. *Ibid.*, 589

The visionary denies the truth to himself, the liar only to others.

Ibid., II, 6

If Christ really intended to redeem the world, may he not be said to have failed? *Ibid.*, 98

If a God created the world, then he must have created a man to be his ape, as a perpetual source of amusement in the midst of his rather tedious eternity.

'The Wanderer and His Shadow', 14

We often preach our faith when we have lost it. *Ibid.*, 66

The Jews took a different view of anger from that held by
others and sanctified it. *Dawn of Day*, 38

The bitterest words ever pronounced, 'My God, my God, why
hath Thou forsaken me?', contain evidence of complete
disillusionment regarding the deceptions of existence.

Ibid., 114

What was once done 'for the love of God' is now done for the
love of money – i.e., that which at present affords us the
highest feeling of power and good conscience. *Ibid.*, 206

God is dead; but there may be millennia to come in which
people will show his shadow in their caves.

Gay Science, 108

In every religion, the religious man is an exception.

Ibid., 128

The whole of religion may appear to some distant age as an
exercise and a prelude. *Ibid.*, 300

Nihilism, the belief in unbelief, always reveals a need for belief,
support, and buttress. *Ibid.*, 347

The struggle against the church is the struggle of the more
ordinary, cheerful, confiding, superficial natures against the
rule of the graver, profounder, more contemplative ones – that
is to say, the more malign and suspicious men who distrust the
worth of life. The ordinary instincts of the people, its sensual
gaiety, its 'good heart', revolts against them. *Ibid.*, 350

The church is under all circumstances a *nobler* institution than
the state. *Ibid.*, 358

For a pious man there is no solitude. *Ibid.*, 367

The creator wished to look away from himself – thereupon he
created the world. *Thus Spake Zarathustra*, III

I could only believe in a God who knew how to dance.

Ibid., VII

Jesus died too early. Had he lived, he would have learned to
love the earth, and laughter too, and would have disavowed
his doctrine. *Ibid.*, XXI

God is a conjecture.   *Ibid.*, XXIV

Since humanity came into being, man has enjoyed himself too
little. That alone is our original sin.   *Ibid.*, XXV

Better to have no God, better to set up destiny on ones's own
account, better to be a fool, better to be God oneself!
                                             Ibid., LXVI

It is a curious thing that God learned Greek when he wished to
turn author – and that he did not learn it better.
                                    Beyond Good and Evil, 121

Christianity gave Eros poison to drink. He did not die of it, but
degenerated into vice.   *Ibid.*, 168

Nihilism harbours in the heart of Christian morals.
                                            Will to Power, 1

Nihilism is the European form of Buddhism, that active
negation after all existence has lost its meaning.   *Ibid.*, 55

Buddhism is the expression of a fine evening, perfectly sweet
and mild. It is a sort of gratitude toward all that lies hidden,
including things it entirely lacks, such as bitterness,
disillusionment and resentment.   *Ibid.*

The Church is precisely what Jesus inveighed against, and
against which He taught His disciples to fight.   *Ibid.*, 168

In the whole of the New Testament, there is not one
bouffonnerie. That fact alone would refute any book.
                                             Ibid., 187

Faith is an asses' bridge.   *Ibid.*, 192

A religion whose objective is to soothe diseased nerves does not
require the terrible solution of a God on the cross. That is why
Buddhism is secretly gaining ground in Europe.   *Ibid.*, 240

Now that faith in God is dead, the question arises once more,
'Who speaks?' My answer, taken from biology, not
metaphysics, is 'the *gregarious instinct speaks*'.   *Ibid.*, 275

Christ died for *his* sins. There is nothing to show that he died
for the sins of others.   *Antichrist*, 27

The gospels lead us into a strange and morbid world which seems to have come from a Russian novel. It is a pity that a Dostoyevsky didn't live in the neighbourhood of this most interesting decadent [Christ]. *Ibid.,* 31

The 'messenger of glad tidings' [Christ] died as he lived – *not* in order to 'save mankind' but to show one how to live.
Ibid., 35

There was never more than one Christian and he *died* on the cross. *Ibid.,* 39

People have always spoken of 'faith' and acted on their instincts. *Ibid.*

When the centre of gravity of life is laid not in life but in a beyond – a *nonentity* – life is robbed of its balance. *Ibid.,* 43

Martyrs have actually harmed the cause of truth. What cause has ever been changed because some one has laid down his life for it? *Ibid.,* 53

Fanatics are picturesque. Mankind prefers to look at poses than to listen to reason. *Ibid.,* 54

What was the glory of the Renaissance? The attempt to transvalue Christian values: to make the opposite values, the *noble* values, triumph. *Ibid.,* 61

A sedentary life is the real sin against the Holy Spirit.
'Why I Am So Clever', 1, *Ecce Homo*

It was God himself who, at the end of His great work, coiled himself up in the form of a serpent at the foot of the tree of knowledge. It was thus that he recovered from being a God. He had made everything too beautiful ... The devil is simply God's moment of idleness, on the seventh day.
'Beyond Good and Evil', *Ibid.,* 2

The concept of 'God' was invented as the opposite of the concept of life. 'Why I Am A Fatality', 8, *Ibid.*

Have you understood me? *Dionysus* versus *Christ!* *Ibid.,* 9

One cannot refute Christianity. It is impossible to refute a diseased eyesight. *Case of Wagner,* Epilogue

Morality

Whatever exists is both just and unjust, and equally justified in both. *Birth of Tragedy*, 9

Morality itself is a symptom of decadence.
Ibid., Appendix, 2

The preaching of a morality is as easy as the establishment of it is difficult. 'David Strauss', VII

When the aim of each of us is centred in another, then no one has an object in existing.
We Philologists, 12

We are from the beginning illogical, and therefore unjust, beings. *Human, All-too-Human*, I, 32

The moral sense must not be lacking in those natures which have no ambition. The ambitious manage without it, with almost the same results. *Ibid.*, 78

When virtue has slept, it will arise again fresher.
Ibid., 83

Morality is the union of the pleasant and the useful.
Ibid., 97

We do not complain of nature as immoral because it sends a thunderstorm and makes us wet. Why then do we call those who injure us immoral? *Ibid.*, 102

The origin of morality may be traced to two ideas: 'The community is of more value than the individual', and 'The permanent interest is to be preferred to the temporary.'
Ibid., II, 89

To most criminals, punishment comes just as illegitimate children come to women. They have done the same thing a hundred times without any bad consequences; suddenly comes discovery, and with it the consequences.
'The Wanderer and His Shadow', 28

Many superior men who have felt urged to throw off the yoke of some morality or other have had no resource but to feign madness, or to actually become insane.

Dawn of Day, 14

Morality is opposed to the formation of new and better morals: it stupefies. *Ibid.*, 19

History deals almost exclusively with *wicked men*, who later come to be recognized as *good men*. *Ibid.*, 20

The Greeks were different from us in the value they set on hope. They saw it as blind and deceitful.

Ibid., 38

The worst diseases of mankind have arisen from the struggle against diseases. *Ibid.*, 52

If you think a thing evil, you make it evil. *Ibid.*, 76

Must we call Eros an enemy? *Ibid.*

Morals are constantly undergoing transformations occasioned by successful crimes. *Ibid.*, 98

To accept a belief simply because it is customary implies that one is dishonest, cowardly and lazy. *Ibid.*, 101

All rules distract our attention from the fundamental aim of the rule and make us more thoughtless. *Ibid.*, 322

Men have become suffering creatures in consequence of their morals. *Ibid.*, 425

'The rule always appears to be more interesting than the exception' – whoever thinks thus has made considerable progress in knowledge, and is one of the initiated.

Ibid., 442

Three-quarters of all the evil committed in the world is due to timidity, and this is above all a physiological process.

Ibid., 538

Narrow souls I hate like the devil,
Souls wherein grows no good nor evil.

'Jest, Ruse and Revenge', 17, *Gay Science*

Every soil becomes exhausted finally, and the ploughshare of
evil must come once more. *Ibid.*, 4

Morality is the herd-instinct in the individual. *Ibid.*, 116

Who is bad? He who always wants to put others to shame.
What is most humane? To spare others shame.
Ibid., 273-4

To sit in judgement morally ought to be opposed to one's taste.
Ibid., 335

Thoughts concerning moral prejudices, if they are not to be
prejudices themselves, presuppose a position outside of
morality. That one should wish to get outside of morality may
be a sort of madness. In any case the question remains whether
one can really get there. *Ibid.*, 380

One virtue is more of a virtue than two, because it is more of a
knot for one's destiny to be tied to.
Thus Spake Zarathustra, Prologue, 4

A little poison now and then – that makes for pleasant dreams.
And much poison at last for a pleasant death. *Ibid.*, 5

You have made danger your calling? There is nothing
contemptible in that. *Ibid.*, 6

What is good, you ask. To be brave is good. *Ibid.*, X

In wickedness, the haughty man and the weakling meet. But
they misunderstand one another. *Ibid.*

A small revenge is more humane than no revenge at all.
Ibid., XIX

To be ashamed of one's immorality is a step on the ladder at
the end of which one is also ashamed of one's morality.
Beyond Good and Evil, 95

What is done out of love always takes place beyond good and
evil. *Ibid.*, 153

Judging morally is the favourite revenge of the intellectually
shallow on those who are less so. It is also an opportunity for
becoming subtle. Malice spiritualizes. *Ibid.*, 219

A grain of wrong pertains even to good taste.

Ibid., 221

Danger is the mother of morality, great danger.   *Ibid.*

Insofar as we believe in morality, we condemn existence.

Will to Power, 6

Overwork, curiosity and sympathy – our modern vices.

Ibid., 73

To be natural means to dare to be as immoral as Nature is.

Ibid., 120

A pang of conscience is a sign that a man's character is not yet equal to his deed.   *Ibid.*, 234

There are no moral phenomena, only moral interpretations of phenomena.   *Ibid.*, 258

In order that a man may respect himself, he must be capable of becoming evil.   *Ibid.*, 288

We immoralists require the power of morality. Our instinct of self-preservation insists upon our opponents maintaining their strength.   *Ibid.*, 361

Morality: a useful error.   *Ibid.*, 402

Belief in morality is not a proof of morality.   *Ibid.*, 445

The object of idealism should be to induce people to do unpleasant things cheerfully.   *Ibid.*, 889

The strongest test of character is to resist being ruined by the seductiveness of goodness. Goodness must be regarded as a luxury, a refinement, a vice.

Ibid., 934

Squandering is typical of genuine goodness. Vital personal wealth is its prerequisite.   *Ibid.*, 935

Pity stinks of the mob. It is next of kin to bad manners.

'Why I Am So Wise', 4, *Ecce Homo*

Psychology

Individuation is the source and primal cause of all suffering.

Birth of Tragedy, 10

Instinct is the creatively affirmative force. Consciousness only comports itself critically and dissuasively. *Ibid.*, 13

In the smallest and the greatest happiness, there is always one thing that makes it happiness: the power of forgetting.

'Uses and Abuses of History', II, *Thoughts Out of Season*, II

Vanity is the involuntary inclination to set oneself up as an individual without really being one. *We Philologists*, 13

There are no institutions which a man should prize more than his own soul. *Ibid.*, 119

When we experience happiness, we are not thinking of ourselves but of our ideal. This lies far off, and only the rapid man attains it. *Ibid.*, 184

In all great deceivers, one thing is noteworthy: their *belief in themselves*. *Human, All-too-Human*, I, 52

Why do most people speak the truth? Because falsehood requires invention, deceit and memory. *Ibid.*, 54

Hope is the worst of all evils, because it prolongs the torments of man. *Ibid.*, 72

Everywhere where there is happiness, there is found pleasure in nonsense. *Ibid.*, 213

Few people will not expose the private affairs of their friends when at a loss for a subject of conversation. *Ibid.*, 327

A profession makes us thoughtless. That is its great blessing. *Ibid.*, 537

Many a man's talent appears less than it is, because he has set himself too heavy tasks. *Ibid.*, 538

Whoever aims at great things and at length perceives that he is too weak to achieve them usually has insufficient strength to renounce his aims publicly and so becomes a hypocrite.

Ibid., 540

Those who seek wit do not possess it. *Ibid.*, 547

We forget our fault when we have confessed it to someone, but he generally does not. *Ibid.*, 568

Opinions evolve out of passions. Indolence of intellect allows these to congeal into convictions. *Ibid.*, 637

The idealist is incorrigible. If he is thrown out of Heaven, he makes a suitable ideal out of Hell.

Ibid., II, 23

The more you let yourself go, the less others let you go.

Ibid., 83

Wit is the epitaph of an emotion. *Ibid.*, 202

Cynicism in intercourse is a sign that, when alone, a man treats himself as a dog. *Ibid.*, 256

The clever man will only make friends with the industrious.

Ibid., 260

Followers never forgive us for taking sides against ourselves, for we seem not only to be spurning their love but also to be exposing them to the charge of lack of intelligence.

Ibid., 309

So long as you are praised, believe that you are not on your own course but on someone else's. *Ibid.*, 340

To lie still and think little is the cheapest medicine for diseases of the soul. *Ibid.*, 361

The sting of conscience, like the gnawing of a dog at a stone, is mere foolishness.

'The Wanderer and His Shadow', 38

He who fortifies himself completely against boredom fortifies himself against himself too. *Ibid.*, 200

When we have found ourselves, we must then learn how from time to time to lose and find ourselves again. – A thinker finds it a drawback always to be tied to one person.

Ibid., 306

Trusting in our feelings simply means obeying our grandfather and grandmother more than the gods within us: our reason and experience.

Dawn of Day, 35

Our so-called consciousness may be a more or less fantastic commentary on an unknown text which is unknowable, yet felt.   *Ibid.*, 119

A man of high rank would do well to develop a gracious memory; to note the good qualities in people and remember them particularly. In this way, he will hold others in agreeable dependence.   *Ibid.*, 278

The friend whose hopes we cannot satisfy we should prefer to have as an enemy.   *Ibid.*, 313

A sick man lives more carelessly when under medical observation than when he attends to his own health.

Ibid., 322

Vanity is the dread of appearing to be original.

Ibid., 365

What can we do to arouse ourselves when we are weary of our ego? Sleep in both the literal and figurative sense of the word.
Ibid., 377

We are like shop-windows where we are constantly arranging, concealing or setting out in front those qualities which others attribute to us – in order to deceive ourselves.

Ibid., 385

One must possess wit and a good conscience to be a knave, and these will almost reconcile the cheated one with the cheat.
Ibid., 388

We begin by unlearning to love others and end by finding nothing lovable in ourselves.

Ibid., 401

Those who are very beautiful, very good and very powerful scarcely ever learn the full truth about anything. In their presence we involuntarily lie.   *Ibid.,* 451

We ought to fear a man who hates himself; for we are liable to become victims of his anger and revenge. Let us then try to tempt him into self-love.   *Ibid.,* 517

We get on with our bad conscience more easily than with our bad reputation.   *Gay Science,* 52

The mere will to health is a prejudice, a cowardice, and perhaps an instance of the subtlest barbarism and unprogressiveness.   *Ibid.,* 120

To laugh means to love mischief, but with a good conscience.
                    Ibid., 200

Either one does not dream at all or one dreams in an interesting manner. One must learn to be awake in the same way – either not at all or in an interesting manner.
                    Ibid., 232

The man who is always thoroughly occupied is rid of all embarrassment.   *Ibid.,* 254

The secret of realizing the largest productivity and the greatest enjoyment of existence is to live dangerously! Build your cities on the slope of Vesuvius.
                    Ibid., 283

We must be able to lose ourselves at times, if we want to learn something of what we do not have in ourselves.
                    Ibid., 305

A defect in personality revenges itself everywhere.
                    Ibid., 280

Great problems all demand *great love.* Only strong, well-rounded, secure spirits – those who have a solid basis – are qualified for them.   *Ibid.*

Great despisers are great adorers.
                    Thus Spake Zarathustra, Prologue, 4

The half-and-half spoil the whole.   *Ibid.,* LII

One should not wish to enjoy where one does not contribute to the enjoyment. And one should not *wish* to enjoy.

Ibid., LVI, 5

All intercourse is bad intercourse save with one's equals.

Beyond Good and Evil, 26

Cynicism is the form in which base souls approach what is called honesty. *Ibid.*

Everything profound loves the mask. *Ibid.*, 54

Under peaceful conditions, the militant man attacks himself.

Ibid., 87

When we have to change an opinion about anyone, we charge heavily to his account the inconvenience he has caused us.

Ibid., 125

The man who fights with monsters should be careful lest he becomes a monster. And if you gaze for too long into the abyss, the abyss will gaze into you.

Ibid., 146

Objection, evasion, joyous distrust and love of irony are signs of health. Everything absolute belongs to pathology.

Ibid., 154

Bad conscience is the illness man was bound to contract once he found himself imprisoned in society and peace.

Genealogy of Morals, II, 16

All instincts which do not find a vent outside of oneself turn inwards. *Ibid.*

Idleness is the parent of all psychology. What? Is psychology then a – *vice*?

'Maxims and Missiles', 1, *Twilight of the Idols*

Culture & Education

Without myth, every culture loses its healthy creative power.
Birth of Tragedy, 28

A people – and also a man – is worth only as much as its ability to impress on its experiences the seal of eternity.
Ibid.

The moment any seeds of real culture are sown, they are in danger of being crushed by the roller of pseudo-culture, journalism.
Future of Our Educational Institutions, I

The education of the masses cannot be our aim, rather the education of a few picked men for great and lasting works.
Ibid., III

Every kind of training which holds out the prospect of bread-winning as its aim is not training for culture as we understand it.
Ibid., IV

Every natural gift must develop itself by contest.
'Homer's Contest', *Early Greek Philosophy*

The weakness of modern personality comes out in the measureless overflow of criticism.
'Uses and Abuses of History', V

Great learning and great shallowness go together very well under one hat.
Ibid., VI

The Philistine detests all education that makes for loneliness, has an aim above money-making, and requires a long time.
'Schopenhauer', VI

A happy age does not need or know the savant. A sick and sluggish time ranks him as its highest and worthiest.
Ibid.

One can live comfortably amid all this modern 'freedom' only if one merely understands it and does not wish to participate in it.
We Philologists, 168

We should study only what we feel we should like to imitate. What is really wanted is a progressive canon of the ideal.

Ibid., 178

Music is the last plant to come up, in the autumn and dying-season of a culture.

Human, All-too-Human, I, 171

Deviating natures are of the utmost importance wherever there is to be progress.   *Ibid.*, 224

Of two quite lofty principles, measure and moderation, it is better not to speak. Most people will imagine the subjects under discussion are tedium and mediocrity.

Ibid., II, 230

Every meal at which we talk well or listen well does harm to the digestion.   'The Wanderer and His Shadow', 203

The machine, itself a product of the highest mental powers, sets in motion hardly any but the lower, unthinking forces.

Ibid., 220

It is because of teachers that so little is learnt, and that so badly.

Ibid., 282

All our poeticizing and thinking from the highest to the lowest is marked by the exaggerated importance placed on the love story as the principal item of our lives.

Dawn of Day, 76

A noble culture may resemble, so far as the passions are concerned, either a horseman who takes pleasure in making his proud and fiery animal trot in the Spanish fashion, or one who feels his horse dart away with him like the elemental forces, so that both horse and rider come close to losing their heads but owing to the enjoyment of the delight attain a new level of strength and clarity.   *Ibid.*, 201

By cautioning his pupils against himself, a teacher shows his humanity.   *Ibid.*, 447

When 'morals decay', those we call tyrants make their appearance. They are the forerunners of the individual and, as it were, early-matured firstlings.

Gay Science, 23

Corruption is only an abusive term for the harvest time of a
people.   *Ibid.*

Man only has value and significance insofar as he is *a stone in a
great building*. For this purpose he must be solid: a stone, and
above all *not* a stage-player.   *Ibid.*, 356

The worst thing a scholar is capable of results from the
mediocrity of his type. He labours instinctively for the
destruction of the exceptional man.

Beyond Good and Evil, 206

Gloominess and pessimistic influence necessarily follow in the
wake of enlightenment.   *Will to Power*, 91

Suffering and symptoms of decline belong to ages of enormous
prejudice.   *Ibid.*, 112

Scientific honesty is always sacrificed when a thinker begins to
reason.   *Ibid.*, 440

The same discipline makes the soldier and the scholar efficient.
Looked at closely, there is no true scholar who does not have
the instincts of the true soldier in him.

Ibid., 912

Education: essentially a means of ruining exceptions in favour
of the rule. Culture: essentially a means of directing taste
against the exceptions in favour of the mediocre.

Ibid., 933

High civilization is a pyramid. It can only stand on a broad
base. Its first prerequisite is a strongly and soundly
consolidated mediocrity.

Antichrist, 57

In the scholar, the instinct of self-defence has decayed;
otherwise he would defend himself against books. The scholar
is a decadent.

'Why I Am So Clever', 8, *Ecce Homo*

The three great stimulants of exhausted people: brutality,
artificiality and innocence.

Case of Wagner, 5

Nations & People

What sufferings the Greeks must have undergone in order to become so beautiful!

Birth of Tragedy, 25

An excess of virtue can bring a nation to ruin as well as an excess of vice.

'Uses and Abuses of History', I

How can anyone glorify and venerate a whole people? It is the individuals that count, even in the case of the Greeks.

We Philologists, 98

In the darkest times of the Middle Ages, it was Jewish free-thinkers, scholars and physicians who upheld the banner of enlightenment and of intellectual independence under the severest personal sufferings, and defended Europe against Asia.   *Human, All-too-Human*, I, 475

Every nation, every individual, has unpleasant and even dangerous qualities. It would be cruel to require the Jews to be an exception.   *Ibid.*

The Greeks were led to art by delight in themselves. Our contemporaries are by disgust in themselves.

Ibid., II, 169

Exceptional Greeks regarded the serious and thorough with a kind of grimace.   *Ibid.*, 221

In Germany, bad writing is looked on as a national privilege.

'The Wanderer and His Shadow', 87

The misfortune of French and German literature of the last hundred years is that the Germans ran away too early from the French school and the French later on went too early to the German.   *Ibid.*, 94

Might not one find among the cultured classes of England, those who read *The Times*, a decline in their powers of sight every ten years?   *Ibid.*, 233

The combination of a martial and industrial spirit, refined manners and Christian severity, has never been more beautifully exhibited than among the Huguenots.

Ibid., 192

Though not at all superficial, a great Frenchman always has his apparent superficiality. On the other hand, the depth of a great German is generally closed up in an ugly-shaped box.

Ibid.

The French free-thinker, in his own inward being, had to fight against truly great men, and not, like the free-thinkers of other nations, merely against dogmas and sublime abortions.

Ibid., 193

The German possesses the secret of knowing how to be tedious in spite of wit, knowledge and feeling.

Ibid.

Their bravery under the cloak of wretched submission, their heroic *spernere se sperni,* is what in the Jews surpasses the virtues of all the saints. *Ibid.,* 205

A German is capable of great things, but he is unlikely to achieve them, for he obeys whenever he can, as suits a naturally lazy intellect. *Ibid.,* 207

Whenever the German *does* reach a state in which he is capable of great things, he invariably raises himself above morals.

Ibid.

Napoleon, as the complete and fully developed type of a single instinct, belongs to ancient humanity, whose characteristics were simple construction, ingenious development and realization of a single or small number of motives.

Ibid., 245

Thomas Carlyle, that arrogant old muddle-head and grumbler, spent his long life trying to romanticize the common sense of his Englishmen – but in vain! *Ibid.,* 298

Stendhal had perhaps the most penetrating eyes and ears of any Frenchman of *this* century. Is it because he had too much of the German and the Englishman in his nature for the Parisians to be able to endure him?

Gay Science, 95

The Jews are the moral genius among nations by virtue of their capacity for despising the human in themselves more than any other people.

Ibid., 136

Socrates – a mocking and amorous demon. The rat-catcher of Athens.

Ibid., 339

Ah, my friends! We must surpass even the Greeks.

Ibid., 340

A nation is a detour of nature to arrive at six or seven great men. Yes, and then to get round them.

Beyond Good and Evil, 126

I have never met a German who was favourably inclined to the Jews; and the repudiation of actual anti-Semitism on the part of prudent and practical men is not directed against the sentiment but against its dangerous excess.

Ibid., 251

What offends in even the humanest Englishman is his lack of music. He has neither rhythm nor dance in the movements of his soul and body – indeed, not even the desire for rhythm and dance. *Ibid.,* 252

The European *noblesse* – of sentiment, taste and manners – is the work and invention of France. The European ignobleness, the plebeianism of modern ideas, is England's work and invention. *Ibid.,* 253

In the French character, there is a successful halfway synthesis between North and South. This preserves them from the dreadful, northern grey-in-grey, from sunless conceptual-spiritism and from poverty of blood – our German infirmities. *Ibid.,* 254

Napoleon – that synthesis of monster and the Superman.
Genealogy of Morals, 56

The higher and better-endowed men will, I hope, turn against Wagner and Schopenhauer. These two Germans flatter our dangerous qualities and are leading us to ruin. A stronger future is prepared in Goethe, Beethoven and Bismarck.

'People and Countries', 12

England's continual change of political parties is a fatal obstacle to the carrying out of any tasks which need to be spread out over a long period of time.

Ibid., 18

Maxim: to associate with no man who takes part in the mendacious race swindle.

Ibid., 21

In the highest types of minds, all things are impelled toward a synthesis of European culture.

Ibid., 23

In Rousseau, there was undoubtedly brain-trouble; in Voltaire, rare health and lightsomeness.

Will to Power, 100

The anti-Semites do not forgive the Jews for having both intellect and money. Anti-Semite – another name for 'bungled and botched'. *Ibid.,* 864

The Revolution made Napoleon possible: that is its justification. Napoleon made nationalism possible: that is its excuse. *Ibid.,* 877

One must be an Englishman to believe that a man always seeks his own advantage.

Ibid., 930

An anti-Semite does not become any more respectable because he lies on principle.

Antichrist, 55

German intellect is indigestion.

'Why I Am So Clever', 1, *Ecce Homo*

The few instances of higher culture I have met in Germany were French in origin.

Ibid., 3

The Greeks were superficial – from *profundity.*

Nietzsche contra Wagner, Epilogue, 2

Philosophy

Unsubdued thirst for knowledge barbarizes just as much as hatred of knowledge.

Early Greek Philosophy, 1

What verse is to the poet, dialectical thinking is to the philosopher. He snatches at it in order to hold fast to his enchantment.

Ibid., 3

Disregard of everything present and momentary lies in the essence of the great philosophic nature.

Ibid., 8

The majesty of truth is not scaled by the rope-ladder of logic.

Ibid., 9

Man conceives of the existence of other things according to the analogy of his own existence ... an illogical transmission.

Ibid., 11

Every idea originates through equating the unequal.

'On Truth and Falsity', *Ibid.*

To value history beyond a certain point mutilates and degrades life.

'Uses and Abuses of History', Preface

His life is the fairest who thinks least about life.

Ibid., II

A modern thinker is always in the throes of an unfulfilled desire. He is looking for life – warm, red life – in order to pass judgment on it.

'Schopenhauer', III

It is infinitely more important that a philosopher should arise than that a state or a university should continue.

Ibid., VIII

There are only three forms of existence in which a man may remain an individual: as a philosopher, as a Saviour, and as an artist.

We Philologists, 118

Mankind as a whole has *no* goals.

Human, All-too-Human, I, 33

Antithesis is the narrow gate through which error is fondest of sneaking to the truth.

Ibid., 187

There has never been a philosopher who has not eventually deprecated the philosophy of his youth.

Ibid., 263

A man who cannot put his thoughts on ice should not enter into the heat of dispute.

Ibid., 315

Convictions are more dangerous enemies of truth than lies.

Ibid., 483

A man who thinks deeply knows he is always in the wrong, however he may act.

Ibid., 518

Belief in truth begins with doubt of all truths in which one has previously believed.

Ibid., II, 20

We are in a prison and can only dream of freedom, not make ourselves free.

Ibid., 33

Many a man fails to become a thinker simply because his memory is too good.

Ibid., 122

If we make truth stand on its head, we generally fail to notice that our own heads are not in their right position either.

Ibid., 208

The philanthropy of the sage sometimes makes him pretend to be excited, enraged or delighted, lest he hurt his surroundings by the coldness and rationality of his nature.

Ibid., 246

Wisdom is the whispering of the sage to himself in a crowded marketplace.

Ibid., 386

An idea can be loved more than a person, and it does not
thwart the lover so often.

'The Wanderer and His Shadow', 232

We should not let ourselves be burnt for our opinions – we are
not so certain of them as all that. But we might let ourselves be
burnt for the right of possessing them.

Ibid., 333

At the end of the search for knowledge, what will men come to
know? Their organs.   *Dawn of Day*, 483

No thinker's thoughts give me so much pleasure as my own.
This of course proves nothing in their favour, but I should be
foolish to neglect fruits which are tasteful only because they
grow on my own tree.   *Ibid.*, 493

The duller the eye so much the further does goodness extend.
Hence the gloominess, allied to bad conscience, of great
thinkers.   *Gay Science*, 53

Man has been reared by his errors   *Ibid.*, 160

Thoughts are the shadows of our sentiments – always
obscurer, emptier and simpler.   *Ibid.*, 179

He is a thinker. That is, he knows how to take things more
simply than they are.   *Ibid.*, 189

Similarizing and equalizing are signs of weak eyes.

Ibid., 228

The thinker does not need applause if he is sure of the clapping
of his own hands.   *Ibid.*, 330

It is best to do with profound problems as with a cold bath –
quickly in, quickly out.   *Ibid.*, 381

The spirit of a philosopher would like nothing better than to be
a good dancer.   *Ibid.*

Not by wrath, but by laughter should we slay.

Thus Spake Zarathustra, VII

Whatever is much thought about is at last thought suspicious.

Ibid., XII

All suppressed truths become poisonous.

Ibid., XXXIV

All truth is crooked. Time itself is a circle.

Ibid., XLVI

Better to know nothing than to half-know many things. Better to be a fool on one's own account than a sage on other people's approbation. *Ibid.*, LXIV

Supposing Truth is a woman – what then?

Beyond Good and Evil, Preface

Without recognition of logical fictions, man could not live. Untruth is a condition of existence.

Ibid., 4

When any one speaks 'badly' of man, the lover of knowledge should perk up his ears.

Ibid., 26

In the search for truth, if a man goes about too humanely, he may find nothing. *Ibid.*, 35

The more abstract the truth you teach, the more you must allure the senses to it. *Ibid.*, 128

Truth is a woman. One must not use force with her.

Ibid., 220

The greatest thoughts are the greatest events.

Ibid., 285

Stoicism of the intellect eventually vetoes negation as rigidly as it does affirmation.

Genealogy of Morals, III, 24

It matters little whether a thing is true provided it is effective.
Will to Power, 172

All ideals are dangerous, because they lower and brand realities. They are poisons, but occasionally indispensable as cures.

Ibid., 223

Philosophers up until now have been contemptible libertines
hiding behind the petticoats of the female 'Truth'.

Ibid., 465

The object ought not to be to 'know', but to schematize: to
impose as much regularity and form upon chaos as our
practical needs require.   *Ibid.,* 515

All human knowledge is either experience or mathematics.

Ibid., 530

In order that truthfulness may be possible, the whole sphere in
which man moves must be very tidy, small and respectable.

Ibid., 543

The will to truth is merely the longing for a stable world.

Ibid., 585, A

The arrogance of man! When he sees no purpose, he denies
there can be one.

Ibid., 599

The formula of happiness? a Yea, a Nay, a straight line, a *goal*.
'Maxims and Missles', 44, *Twilight of the Idols*

Great minds are sceptical. Convictions are prisons.

Antichrist, 54

To comprehend the limits of reason – this alone is genuine
philosophy.   *Ibid.,* 55

All idealism is falsehood in the face of necessity.
'Why I Am So Clever', 10, *Ecce Homo*

What is the first and last thing a philosopher demands from
himself? To overcome his age in himself, to become 'timeless'.
With what then does the philosopher have the greatest fight?
With all that makes him a child of his time.

Case of Wagner, Preface

The philosopher must be the evil conscience of his age – but to
this end he must have its best knowledge.   *Ibid.*

Perhaps truth is a woman who has reasons for not revealing
her reasons?   *Nietzsche contra Wagner,* Epilogue, 2

Politics

Only those who stand outside the political instincts know what they want from the State.

'The Greek State', *Early Greek Philosophy*

Objectivity and justice have nothing to do with one another.

'Uses and Abuses of History', VI

We are feeling the consequences of the doctrine preached lately from all the housetops that the State is the highest end of man, and that there is no higher duty than to serve it. I regard this as a lapse not into paganism, but into stupidity.

'Schopenhauer', IV

The man with the *furor philosophicus* in him will no longer have time for the *furor politicus*, and will wisely keep from reading the newspapers or serving a party.

Ibid., VII

All states are managed badly when men other than politicians busy themselves with politics, and they deserve to be ruined by these amateurs.

Ibid., VIII

The better the state is organized, the duller humanity will be.

We Philologists, 192

Gradually increasing stupidity follows all stability like its shadow.

Human, All-too-Human, I, 224

To be a law-giver is a sublimated form of tyranny.

Ibid., 261

All mankind is divided as it always has been into slaves and freemen. Whoever has less than two-thirds of his day for himself is a slave, be he a statesman, a merchant, an official or a scholar.

Ibid., 283

Against war, it should be said that it makes the victor stupid and the vanquished revengeful.

Ibid, 444

Culture is indebted most of all to politically weakened periods.
Ibid., 465

In large states, public education will always be mediocre for
the same reason that cooking is mediocre in large kitchens.
Ibid., 467

In all institutions into which the sharp breeze of public
criticism does not penetrate, an innocent corruption grows up
like a fungus.   *Ibid.,* 468

Modern democracy is the historical form of the decay of the
State.   *Ibid.*

Socialism is the fantastic younger brother of an almost decrepit
despotism, which it wants to succeed.
Ibid., 473

Public opinion – private laziness.   *Ibid.,* 482

When an invincible desire to obtain tyrannical power has been
awakened in the soul, even a mediocre talent gradually
becomes an almost irresistible natural force.   *Ibid.,* 530

Whoever thinks much is unsuitable as a party-man. His
thinking will lead him too quickly beyond the party.
Ibid., 579

The doctrine of free will is an invention of the ruling classes.
'The Wanderer and His Shadow', 9

The robber and the man of power who promises to protect a
community from robbers are at bottom beings of the same
mould, but the latter attains his ends by other means than the
former – by regular imposts paid to him by the community
and no longer by forced contributions.
Ibid., 22

Weariness is the shortest path to equality and fraternity – and
finally liberty is bestowed by sleep.
Ibid., 263

Democratic institutions are centres of quarantine against the
old plague of tyrannical desires. As such, they are extremely
useful and extremely tedious.
Ibid., 289

Work – that is, severe toil from morning to night – serves as the best police. It effectively hinders the development of reason, greed and the desire for independence.

Dawn of Day, 173

AS LITTLE STATE AS POSSIBLE! *Ibid.*, 179

Some people govern because of their passion for governing, others in order that they may not be governed. The latter choose it as the lesser of two evils. *Ibid.*, 181

People will always obey, provided that they can become intoxicated in doing so. *Ibid.*, 188

Neither necessity nor desire, but the love of power, is the demon of mankind. *Ibid.*, 262

The same men who aspire most ardently to power feel it indescribably agreeable to be overpowered. *Ibid.*, 271

Despots like those countries where the weather is moral.

Ibid.

Honesty is the great temptress of all fanatics.

Ibid., 511

Truth in itself is no power. It must either attract power to its side or else side with power, or it will perish again and again.

Ibid., 535

Conservatives of all times are adventitious liars.

Gay Science, 29

Politics may one day be found to be so vulgar as to be described, along with all party and daily journalism, under the rubric: 'Prostitution of the intellect.' *Ibid.*, 31

Liberality is often merely a form of timidity in the rich.

Ibid., 199

Is it not necessary for a man who wants to move the multitude to give a stage-representation of himself?

Ibid., 236

No conqueror believes in chance. *Ibid.*, 258

Power likes to walk on crooked legs.

Thus Spake Zarathustra, II

Many too many are born. The state was devised for the
superfluous ones. *Ibid.*, XI

Insanity in individuals is something rare. In groups, parties,
nations and epochs, it is the rule.

Beyond Good and Evil, 156

The time for petty politics is past. The next century will bring a
struggle for dominion of the world – the *compulsion* to great
politics. *Ibid.*, 208

There will always be too many people of property for
socialism to signify anything more than an attack of illness.

Will to Power, 125

Socialism, like a restless mole beneath the foundations of a
society wallowing in stupidity, will be able to achieve
something useful. It will delay 'Peace on Earth' and the process
of character-softening in the democratic herding animal. It will
force the European to develop an extra supply of craft and
caution and will prevent him from entirely abandoning manly
and warlike qualities. It will also save Europe awhile from the
marasmus femininus which is threatening it.

Ibid.

The type of perfection in politics is, of course,
Machiavellianism. *Ibid.*, 304

Everything that a man does in service to the state is against his
own nature. *Ibid.*, 718

There is no relationship between work done and money
received. The individual should be placed so as to perform the
highest that is compatible with his powers. *Ibid.*, 763

People demand freedom only when they have no power. Once
power is obtained, a preponderance of it is sought. If this is not
achieved, then 'justice', i.e. 'equality of power', becomes the
object of desire. *Ibid.*, 784

The polite term for mediocre is the word 'Liberal'.

Ibid., 864

Women, Love & Family

There is a good deal of curiosity even in maternal love.

Human, All-too-Human, I, 363

The best friend will probably get the best wife, because a good marriage is based on talent for friendship.

Ibid., 378

Whoever has not got a good father should procure one.

Ibid., 381

The surest remedy for the male disease of self-contempt is the love of a sensible woman. *Ibid., 384*

Some mothers need happy and honoured children, some need unhappy ones – otherwise they will not be able to exhibit their maternal excellence. *Ibid., 387*

Some husbands have sighed over the elopement of their wives. The greater number, however, have sighed because nobody would elope with theirs. *Ibid., 388*

Women can enter into friendship with a man perfectly well; but in order to maintain it, the aid of a little physical antipathy is required. *Ibid., 390*

If married couples did not live together, happy marriages would be more frequent. *Ibid., 393*

All intercourse which does not elevate a man debases him.

Ibid., 394

Through love, women actually become what they appear to be in the imagination of their lovers.

Ibid., 400

Everything in marriage is transitory except talk, which occupies most of the association. *Ibid., 406*

Women's vanity requires a man to be something more than just a happy husband. *Ibid., 407*

Women have intelligence; men have character and passion.
Ibid., 411

It is a sign of women's wisdom that they have always known how to get themselves supported.   *Ibid.*, 412

The best women cherish in their breasts a secret scorn for science, as if they were superior to it.   *Ibid.*, 416

After a personal quarrel between a man and a woman, the former suffers chiefly from the idea of having wounded the other, while the latter suffers chiefly from the idea of not having wounded the other enough. Thus she will endeavour by tears, sobs and discomposed mien to make his heart even heavier.   *Ibid.*, 420

Marriage is a necessary institution for one's twenties and a useful, but not necessary one for the thirties. For later life it is often harmful and promotes a man's mental deterioration.
Ibid., 421

In matters of the highest philosophy, all married men are suspect.   *Ibid.*, 436

The demand to be loved is the greatest of presumptions.
Ibid., 523

Love desires, fear avoids.   *Ibid.*, 603

In order to become beautiful, a woman must not desire to be considered pretty.   *Ibid.*, 292

Stupidity in a woman is unfeminine.
'The Wanderer and His Shadow', 273

At a time when a man is in love, he should not be allowed to come to a decision about his life or to determine once and for all the character of his society.   *Dawn of Day*, 151

How many a man has awakened one morning to the realization that his wife is dull, though she thinks the contrary? And then there are those wives whose flesh is willing, but whose intellect is weak.   *Ibid.*, 294

Is there a more sacred state than that of pregnancy?
Ibid., 552

Love is perhaps the most unqualified expression of egoism.
Gay Science, 14

Love pardons even the passion of the beloved.   *Ibid.*, 62

Older women are more sceptical in the recesses of their hearts
than men are. They believe in the superficiality of existence,
and all virtue and profundity is to them only a disguising of
this 'truth' – an affair of modesty and nothing more.
Ibid., 64

Wives easily feel their husbands to be a question-mark to their
honour, and their children as an apology or atonement.
Ibid., 71

Women fail of success when they become agitated and
uncertain and talk too much in the presence of the man they
love. Men are most successfully seduced by subtle and
phlegmatic tenderness.   *Ibid.*, 74

Fathers and sons are much more considerate of one another
than mothers and daughters.   *Ibid.*, 221

Love also has to be learned.   *Ibid.*, 334

A man who loves like a woman becomes thereby a slave. A
woman who loves like a woman becomes thereby a more
perfect woman.   *Ibid.*, 363

Woman wants to be taken and accepted as a possession.
Consequently she wants one who *takes*.   *Ibid.*

A more subtle and jealous thirst for possession is what makes a
man's love continue.   *Ibid.*

One must know how to be a sponge if one would be loved by
overflowing hearts.
Thus Spake Zarathustra, XVI0

Man is for woman a means; the purpose is always a child. But
what is woman for man?
Ibid., XVIII

The true man wants two things: danger and diversion.
Therefore he wants woman, the most dangerous plaything.
Ibid.

Woman understands children better than man, but man is more childish than woman.

Ibid.

Man in his innermost soul is merely evil. Woman, however, is mean. *Ibid.*

Happiness runs after me. That is because I do not run after women. Happiness, however, is a woman.

Ibid., XLVII

Only the man who is man enough will save the woman in woman. *Ibid.*, XLIX

Where one can no longer love, there one should *pass by!*
Ibid., LI

I would have man fit for war and woman fit for maternity. Both, however, should be fit for dancing, with head as well as with legs. *Ibid.*, LVI

Better marriage-breaking than marriage-bending and lying.
Ibid.

The badly-paired are the most revengeful. They make everyone suffer for the fact that they are no longer single.
Ibid.

The same emotions are in man and in woman, but in different *tempi*. Because of this, men and women never cease to misunderstand one another.

Beyond Good and Evil, 85

One ultimately loves one's desires, not the thing desired.
Ibid., 175

We learn to *despise* when we love, and precisely when we love best. *Ibid.*, 216

On the whole, 'woman' has been most despised by woman herself and not by men. *Ibid.*, 232

Wherever the industrial spirit has triumphed over the military and aristocratic, woman strives for the economic and legal independence of a clerk. *Ibid.*, 239

Since the French Revolution the influence of woman has *declined* in proportion as she has increased her rights and claims.   *Ibid.*

For lovers in the real and strong meaning of the term, the satisfaction of sexual desire is inessential. It is merely a symbol.
Will to Power, 732

As a counter-agent to prostitution, or as its ennoblement, I would recommend leasehold marriages. These could last for a term of years or of months, with adequate provision for the children.   *Ibid.*, 733

What is it that pleases almost all pious women, old or young? A saint with beautiful legs, still young, still innocent.
Ibid., 800

Self-admiration is healthy. Has a beautiful woman who knew she was well-dressed ever caught cold?
Ibid., 807

When a man loves, he is a good liar about himself and to himself. He seems to himself transfigured, stronger, richer, more perfect. He is more perfect.
Ibid., 808

The distinguishing qualities between the sexes must be developed more and more. The gulf between them must be made ever wider.
Ibid., 886

The perfect woman tears you to pieces when she loves you.
'Why I Write Such Excellent Books', 5, *Ecce Homo*

The more womanly a woman is the more she fights tooth and nail against rights in general. The natural order of things, the eternal war between the sexes, assigns her by far the foremost rank.   *Ibid.*

What becomes of the 'eternal Jew' whom a woman adores and enchains? He simply ceases from being eternal. He marries – that is to say, he concerns us no more.
Ibid.

Language & Literature

Among many thousands, perhaps *one* is justified in describing himself as literary. All others who at their own risk try to be so deserve to be met with Homeric laughter.

Future of Educational Institutions, II

Every so-called classical education has only one natural starting-point – an artistic, earnest and exact familiarity with the use of the mother-tongue; this together with the secret of form.   *Ibid.*

The proof of a good style is how easily it may be translated into Latin.   *Ibid.*

Paradoxes are only assertions that carry no conviction. The author has made them wishing to appear brilliant or to mislead or above all to pose.   'Schopenhauer', II

The joyfulness one finds here and there in mediocre writers and limited thinkers makes higher spirits miserable.   *Ibid.*

All writing is useless that does not contain a stimulus to activity.   *Ibid.*, VIII

To have written a single line which is deemed worthy of being commented upon by scholars of a later time far outweighs the merits of the greatest critic.

We Philologists, 67

Philologists stand in the same relation to true educators as the medicine men of the wild Indians do to true physicians.

Ibid., 71

A good author possesses not only his own intellect but also that of his friends.

Human, All-too-Human, I, 180

The misfortune of acute and clear authors is that people consider them shallow and therefore do not devote effort to them. The good fortune of obscure writers is that the reader makes an effort to understand them and gives them the credit for his own zeal.   *Ibid.*, 181

The so-called paradoxes of an author to which a reader objects are often not in the author's book at all, but in the reader's head.   *Ibid.,* 185

The wittiest authors produce a scarcely noticeable smile.
                                                                Ibid., 186

Most thinkers write badly because they communicate not only their thoughts but also the thinking of them.
                                                                Ibid., 188

The best author will be he who is ashamed to become one.
                                                                Ibid., 192

To look on writing as a regular profession should be regarded as a form of madness.   *Ibid.,* 194

There will always be a need of bad authors.   *Ibid.,* 201

In order to interest clever persons in a theory, it is sometimes only necessary to put it before them in the form of a prodigious paradox.   *Ibid.,* 307

The habit of irony, like that of sarcasm, spoils the character. It gradually fosters the quality of a malicious superiority. One finally grows like a snappy dog that has learnt to laugh as well as to bite.   *Ibid.,* 372

One should only speak where one cannot remain silent, and only speak of what one has *conquered* – the rest is all chatter, 'literature' or bad breeding.

                                                Ibid., II, Preface, 1

It is a disadvantage for good thoughts when they follow too closely on one another, for they hide the view from each other. That is why great artists and writers have made an abundant use of the mediocre.   *Ibid.,* 120

When his book opens its mouth, the author must shut his.
                                                                Ibid., 140

All poets and men of letters who are in love with the superlative want to do more than they can.   *Ibid.,* 141

A book is made better by good readers and clearer by good opponents.   *Ibid.,* 153

The mediocre and bad book is mediocre and bad because it seeks to please a great number.

Ibid., 158

Every word is a preconceived judgment.

'The Wanderer and His Shadow', 55

Real thoughts of real poets always go about with a veil on, like Egyptian women.

Ibid., 105

Pithy conciseness, repose and maturity – where you find these qualities in an author, cry halt and celebrate a great festival in the desert.   *Ibid.,* 108

An excellent quotation may spoil whole pages, even a whole book. It seems to cry warningly to the reader, 'I am the precious stone and round me is pale, worthless lead!'

Ibid., 111

I will never again read an author of whom one can suspect that he *wanted* to make a book, but only those writers whose thoughts unexpectedly became a book.

Ibid., 121

A stubborn avoidance of convention means a desire not to be understood. What then is the object of the modern craze for originality?   *Ibid.,* 122

There may come an elevated stage of humanity in which the Europe of the peoples is a dark, forgotten thing, but Europe lives on in thirty books, very old but never antiquated – in the classics.   *Ibid.,* 125

The use of neologisms or archaisms, the preference for the rare and the bizarre, the attempt to enrich rather than to limit the vocabulary, are always signs either of an immature or of a corrupted taste.

Ibid., 127

Improving our style means improving our ideas, and nothing else.

Ibid., 131

More depends on what things are called than on what they are.

Gay Science, 96

Prose is an uninterrupted, polite warfare with poetry. All its charm consists in the fact that poetry is constantly avoided and contradicted.

Ibid., 126

Warfare is the father of all good things. It is also the father of good prose.

Ibid.

Q: Why do you write? A: Well, Sir, I have hitherto found no other means of getting rid of my thoughts.

Ibid., 127

Of what account is a book that never carries us away beyond all books?

Ibid., 205

I love only what is written with blood. Write with blood and you will find that blood is spirit.

Thus Spake Zarathustra, VII

Nowadays the text often disappears under the interpretation.

Beyond Good and Evil, 38

In the beginning, images; then, words; finally, concepts.

Will to Power, 506

Compared with music, communication by means of words is a shameless mode of procedure. Words reduce and stultify. Words make impersonal. Words make common that which is uncommon.

Ibid., 810

English genius vulgarizes and makes realistic all it sees. The French whittles down, simplifies, rationalizes, embellishes. The German muddles, compromises, involves, and infects everything with morality. The Italian genius is the richest and has the most to bestow.

Ibid., 831

How is decadence characterized in literature? By the fact that life no longer animates the whole. Words become predominant.

Case of Wagner, 7

Strength & The Life Force

Strength can manifest itself originally only in speed.
Early Greek Philosophy, 18

How wretched, shadow-like, transitory, purposeless and
fanciful the human intellect appears in Nature.
'On Truth and Falsity', *Ibid.*

Forgetfulness is a property of all action.
'Uses and Abuses of History', I

To live is ever to be in danger.   'Schopenhauer', III

Nature needs the artist, as she needs the philosopher, for a
metaphysical end: to explain herself.
Ibid., V

Nature always desires the greatest utility but does not
understand how to find the best and handiest means to her
end. That is her great sorrow and the cause of her melancholy.
Ibid., VII

Few motives, energetic action and a good conscience compose
what is called strength of character.
Human, All-too-Human, I, 228

It is the misfortune of the active that their activity is almost
always a little senseless.
Ibid., 283

We are so fond of being out in Nature, because it has no
opinions about us.
Ibid., 508

Humanity ruthlessly uses every individual as material for the
heating of its great machines. What then is the purpose of the
machines, when individuals are useful only to maintain them?
Ibid., 585

All rejection and negation betoken a deficiency in fertility.
Ibid., II, 352

Eternal vigour of life is the important point. What matters 'eternal life', or indeed life at all?

Ibid., 408

Among human beings, there is no greater banality than death. Second comes birth, and next comes marriage. So much depends on new actors, so little on the piece.

'The Wanderer and His Shadow', 58

How is it that health is less contagious than disease – particularly in matters of taste? Or are there epidemics of health? *Ibid.*, 129

Evolution does not make happiness its goal. It aims at evolution and nothing else.

Dawn of Day, 108

If a man wishes to act the hero on stage, he must not think of forming part of the chorus. He should not even know how the chorus is made up. *Ibid.*, 177

The dying man has probably lost in life things which were more important than he is now about to lose by death.

Ibid., 349

A powerful mildness as that of a father – wherever this feeling takes possession of man, there he should build his house, whether it is in the midst of the multitude or on some silent spot. *Ubi pater sum, ibi patria.* *Ibid.*, 473

To hear everyday what is said about us, or even to endeavour to discover what people think, will in the end destroy even the strongest man. *Ibid.*, 522

The poison by which the weaker nature is destroyed is strengthening to the strong individual – and he does not call it poison. *Gay Science*, 19

Living – would that mean to continually eliminate from ourselves what is about to die; to be cruel to all that becomes weak and old; to be without pity toward the wretched?

Ibid., 26

Let us be on guard against saying there are laws in nature. There are only necessities.

Ibid., 109

The greatest charm of life is that it puts a gold-embroidered veil of potentialities over itself, promising, resisting, modest, mocking, sympathetic, seductive. Yes, life is a woman!

Ibid., 339

The will to power is just the will to live. *Ibid.,* 349

One must learn to die at the right time.

Thus Spake Zarathustra, XXI

Life strives to rise, and in rising to surpass itself.

Ibid., XXIX

Where is innocence? Where there is will to procreation.

Ibid., XXXVIII

Whatever has become perfect, everything mature, wants to die.

Ibid., LXXIX

Joy does not want heirs – it wants itself, it wants eternity, it wants recurrence, it wants everything eternally like itself.

Ibid.

We must not desire one state only. We must rather desire to be periodical creatures – like existence.

Ibid., notes, 70

Is not life a hundred times too short for us – to bore ourselves?

Beyond Good and Evil, 227

At the core of all aristocratic races lurks the beast of prey; the magnificent *blonde brute*, avid for spoil and victory.

Genealogy of Morals, I, 11

It is not from the strongest that harm comes to the strong, but from the weakest.

Ibid., III, 14

All that is done in weakness ends in failure. Moral: when in a weak position, do nothing. Unfortunately, it is precisely strength that is required in order to stop action.

Will to Power, 45

If Life had a final purpose, it would have been reached already.

Ibid., 55

There is no such thing as egoism which keeps within its
bounds.   *Ibid.*, 369

Are there really such things as will, purposes, thoughts,
values? Is the whole of conscious life perhaps no more than a
mirage?   *Ibid.*, 676

Man as a species does not represent any progress compared
with any other animal. The whole of the animal and plant
world does not develop from the lower to the higher but all
simultaneously, haphazardly, confusedly, and at variance.
                                                           Ibid., 684

The 'wild' man (or in moral terms, the *evil* man) is a reversion
to Nature – and in a certain sense, he represents a recovery, a
cure from the effects of 'culture'.
                                                           Ibid.

There is no such thing as a right to live, a right to work, or a
right to be happy. In this respect, man is not different from the
meanest worm.   *Ibid.*, 759

Great well-being arises from contemplating Nature's
indifference to good and evil.
                                                           Ibid., 850

Generally, a preference for questionable and terrible things is a
symptom of strength.   *Ibid.*, 852

How does one become stronger? By deciding slowly, and by
holding firmly to the decision once it is made.
                                                           Ibid., 918

Everything happens just as it ought to happen.
                                                           Ibid., 1004

Everything becomes and returns for ever. Escape is impossible.
                                                           Ibid., 105

The universe is a monster of energy, without beginning or end.
                                                           Ibid., 1067

Species do not evolve toward perfection. The weak always
prevail over the strong, simply because they are the majority
and because they are more crafty.
        'Skirmishes in a War with the Age', 14, *Twilight of the Idols*

Eternal life, the eternal recurrence of life, the future promised
and hallowed in the past; the triumphant Yea to life despite
death and change; real life conceived as a collective
prolongation through procreation, through the mysteries of
sexuality – I know of no higher goal that these principles of the
cult of Dionysus.

'Things I Owe to the Ancients', 4, *Ibid.*

Man is the great *arrière pensée* of evolution. By no means the
'crown of creation', he is, relatively speaking, the most botched
and diseased of animals, having wandered furthest from his
instincts.

Antichrist, 14

If all the possible combinations and relations of forces had not
already been exhausted, then an infinity would not yet lie
behind us. But since an infinite past must be assumed, no fresh
possibility can exist and everything must have appeared
already – indeed, an infinite number of times.

Eternal Recurrence (a fragment), 7

Let us guard against believing that the universe has a tendency
to attain certain forms – to become more beautiful, more
perfect, more complicated. All that is anthropomorphism.

Ibid., 22

Our world consists of the ashes of an incalculable number of
living creatures.

Ibid., 23

The world of energy suffers no diminution. Otherwise, with
eternal time, it would have grown weak and finally have
perished altogether.

Ibid., 25

What has been the greatest objection to life up to now? – God.

'Why I Am So Clever', 3, *Ecce Homo*

Genius & Greatness

Education is first and foremost obedience and submission to the discipline of genius.

Future of Educational Institutions, IV

Simplicity in style is ever the sign of genius. It alone has the privilege of expressing itself naturally and guilelessly.

'David Strauss', X

Every really productive thing is offensive. *Ibid.*, XI

For an event to be great, two things must be united – the lofty sentiment of those who accomplish it, and the lofty sentiment of those who witness it.

'Wagner at Bayreuth', I

No happy course of life is open to the genius. He stands in contradiction to his age and must perforce struggle with it.

We Philologists, 115

An unceasing desire to create is vulgar. If a man *is* something, it is not necessary for him to *do* anything. And yet he does a great deal. *Human, All-too-Human*, I, 210

A superior mind takes pleasure in the tactlessness, pretentiousness and even hostility of ambitious youths. It is the vicious habit of fiery horses which have not yet carried a rider, but in a short time will be proud to do so. *Ibid.*, 339

Whoever wants to set a good example must add a grain of folly to his virtue. People then imitate their exemplar and at the same time raise themselves above him, a thing they love to do.

Ibid., 561

Original minds are distinguished not by being the first to see a new thing but by seeing the old, well-known thing which is overlooked as something new.

Ibid., II, 200

The highest men act out their lives without keeping back any residue of inner experience. *Ibid.*, 228

What is genius? To aspire to a lofty aim and to will the means to achieve it.   *Ibid.,* 378

The followers of a great man often put their own eyes out so that they may be better able to sing his praises.

Ibid., 390

Only the highest and most active animals are capable of being bored.

'The Wanderer and His Shadow', 56

The thinker needs no one to refute him. He is quite capable of doing that himself.   *Ibid.,* 249

The great man intercedes in favour of unassuming things.

Dawn of Day, 434

A defect in character may become the school of genius.

Ibid., 452

So long as genius dwells within us we are full of audacity – indeed, almost mad, and heedless of health, life and honour. But let genius once leave us and we are instantly overcome by a feeling of the most profound despondency.

Ibid., 538

Whenever a great thinker tries to make himself a lasting institution for posterity, we may readily suppose that he has passed the climax of his powers and is very tired and near the setting of his sun.

Ibid., 542

I praise leaders and forerunners: that is to say, those who leave themselves behind and do not care in the least whether anyone is following them or not.

Ibid., 554

The higher we soar, the smaller we appear to those who cannot fly.   *Ibid.,* 574

Rare men would rather perish than work without delight in their labour.   *Gay Science,* 42

The great man is cruel to his second-rate virtues and judgements.   *Ibid.,* 266

Greatness requires that one not perish from internal distress or doubt when one inflicts great anguish.

Ibid., 250

I teach you the Superman. Man is something that is to be surpassed.

Thus Spake Zarathustra, Prologue, 1

One must have chaos in one to give birth to a dancing star.

Ibid.

Now is the great noontide, when man is in the middle of his course between animal and Superman.

Ibid., XXII

For a tree to become great, it seeks to twine hard roots around hard rocks.

Ibid., XLIX

My suffering and my fellow-suffering – what do they matter? Do I strive after *happiness*? I strive after my *work*.

Ibid., LXXX

The destiny of the higher man is to be a creator.   *Ibid.*, 74

The man who attains his ideal precisely thereby surpasses it.

Beyond Good and Evil, 73

A man of genius is unbearable unless he possesses at least two things besides: gratitude and purity.

Ibid., 74

Is greatness possible – nowadays?   *Ibid.*, 212

Egoism belongs to the essence of a noble soul.   *Ibid.*, 265

Profound suffering ennobles. It separates.   *Ibid.*, 270

Heroism is no form of selfishness, for one is shipwrecked by it.

'People and Countries', 26

We can conceive of nothing great which does not involve a great crime. All greatness is associated in our minds with a certain standing-beyond-the-pale in morality.

Will to Power, 120

Through modesty, many of the choicest intellects perish.
Ibid., 326

Genius lies in the instincts; goodness does too. One only acts perfectly when one acts instinctively.
Ibid., 440

The only thing today which proves whether a man has any value is *his capacity for sticking to his guns.*
Ibid., 910

What does one repent most? One's modesty.   *Ibid.*, 918

All freedom of spirit – i.e., instinctive scepticism – is a prerequisite for greatness.
Ibid., 963

We must not let ourselves be seduced by blue eyes and heaving breasts. Greatness of soul has nothing romantic about it. And unfortunately nothing amiable either.
Ibid., 980

Terribleness belongs to greatness: let us not deceive ourselves.
Ibid., 1028

Those who have been deeply wounded have the Olympian laughter.   *Ibid.*, 1040

Great words and great attitudes are so becoming to decadents.
'Things I Owe to the Ancients', 3, *Twilight of the Idols*

Every conquest, every step forward in knowledge, is the outcome of courage, hardness to one's self and cleanliness.
Ecce Homo, Preface, 3

Genius is conditioned by dry air, by a pure sky.
'Why I Am So Clever', 2, *Ibid.*

The formula for greatness in man is *amor fati.*
Ibid., 10

A man pays dearly for being immortal. To this end, he must die many times over during his life.
Ibid., on *Thus Spake Zarathustra*, 5

The Free Spirit

The free spirit is brought into disrepute chiefly by scholars, who miss their thoroughness and ant-like industry in his art of regarding things and would gladly banish him into a single corner of science.

Human, All-too-Human, I, 282

The man who has attained intellectual emancipation to any extent cannot, for very long, regard himself as other than a wanderer on the face of the earth – and not even as a traveller towards a final goal, for there is no such thing. But he certainly wants to observe and keep his eyes open to whatever actually happens in the world; therefore he cannot attach his heart too firmly to anything individual. He must have in himself something that takes pleasure in change and transitoriness.

Ibid., 406

In solitude a man is eaten up by himself, in crowds by others. Choose which you prefer.

Ibid, II, 348

Every man is himself a piece of fate.

'The Wanderer and His Shadow', 229

Whoever proceeds on his own path meets nobody. That is the feature of one's 'own path'.

Dawn of Day, Preface

The great problems can be picked up in the highways and byways.

Ibid., 127

The doctrine of free will has as its parents man's pride and sense of power.

Ibid., 128

I hate to follow and I hate to lead.
Obedience? no! and ruling? no, indeed!

'Jest, Ruse and Revenge', 33, *Gay Science*

The praise of unselfish virtues is injurious to the individual. It elevates impulses which deprive him of his noblest self-love and the power to take best care of himself.

Ibid., 21

For an inventive spirit, ennui is the unpleasant calm of the soul which precedes the happy voyage and dancing breezes. He must endure it; he must await the effect of it on him. It is precisely *this* which lesser natures cannot experience.

Ibid., 42

Saint and witch together prancing,
Let us foot it up and down.

'Songs of Prince Free-as-a-Bird', *Ibid.*

Be on guard against the good and the just. They hate the lonesome ones.

Thus Spake Zarathustra, XVII

The spirit of all free spirits is the laughing storm.

Ibid., LXXIII

All free spirits who are not on guard against magicians will lose their freedom.

Ibid., LXXV

The ego is a *primum mobile*.   *Ibid.*, notes, 38

Loneliness for a certain time is necessary in order that a creature may become completely permeated with his own soul – cured and hard.

Ibid., 54

The manner in which the Superman must live: like an Epicurean God.

Ibid., 77

The unity in power of the creator, the lover and the knight of knowledge ...

Ibid., 79

Our body is but a social structure composed of many souls.

Beyond Good and Evil, 29

It is the business of the few to be independent. It is a privilege of the strong.

Ibid.

One must know how to conserve oneself – the best test of independence.

Ibid., 41

All society makes one somehow, somewhere, sometime 'commonplace'.

Ibid., 284

We immortalize what cannot live and fly much longer.

Ibid., 296

For some time past there have been no free spirits. They still believe in truth.

Genealogy of Morals, III, 24

It is no small advantage to have a hundred swords of Damocles suspended over one. It is only thus that one learns to dance.

Will to Power, 770

The aim should be to prepare for a *transvaluation of all values* for a particularly strong kind of man, most highly gifted in intellect and will, and to this end slowly and cautiously to liberate in him a host of slandered instincts previously held in check.

Ibid., 957

I am writing for a race of men which does not exist yet: for the lords of the earth.

Ibid., 958

Away from rulers and rid of all bonds live the highest men. And in the rulers they have their instruments.

Ibid., 998

The day after tomorrow belongs to me. Some are born posthumously.

Antichrist, Preface

We free spirits are already a 'transvaluation of all values', an incarnate declaration of war against the old concepts of 'true' and 'untrue'.

Ibid., 13

Let us stamp the impress of eternity upon our lives! This thought contains more than all the religions.

Eternal Recurrence (a fragment), 35

A Claude Lorrain extended to infinity, each day equal to the last in its wild perfection ...

Ecce Homo, on *Twilight of the Idols*, 3

I am not a man. I am dynamite.

'Why I am a Fatality', 1, *Ibid.*

La gaya scienza: light feet, wit, fire, grave, grand logic, stellar dancing, wanton intellectuality, the vibrating light of the South, the calm sea – perfection ...

Case of Wagner, 10